LOW CALORIE TREATS

MANDY ROBERTS

WARNING

You should consult your own doctor before starting this or any other serious diet.

Never go on an unsupervised diet if you weigh less than your recommended weight for height.

We all need some fat in our diets. Fat soluble vitamins and essential fatty acids make fat vital for healthy living.

Children and older people need a larger percentage of fats in their diets. Children under five should always have full fat milk and butter and **not** low fat alternatives.

Published by
Boatswain Press Ltd
Dudley House, 12 North Street
Emsworth, Hampshire PO10 7DQ

Cover design, Slatter Anderson
Printed in Great Britain

British Library Cataloguing-in-Publication Data
A catalogue record for this book is available from the British Library
ISBN 1 873432 24 0

Contents

LOW CALORIE TREATS

Sole with orange sauce and crepes	67
Fat free roast potatoes	69
Creamed potatoes	70
Nutty mashed potatoes	70
Chips	71
Potato pancakes	71
Ratatouille	72
Low calorie pastry	73
Treacle tart	73
Strawberry pavlova	75
Raspberry mousse	76
Bakewell tart	76
Chocolate ice cream	78
Black cherry cheesecake	79
Christmas pudding	80
Low calorie brandy butter	82
Mango and passion fruit sorbet	82
Low calorie custard	84
Pancakes	85
Chocolate pancakes	86
Toffee bananas	87
The ten minute birthday cake	88
Chocolate walnut cake	89
Rice pudding with almonds	90
Pear sorbet	91
Strawberry ice cream	92
Celery and ham sauce	92
Low calorie white sauce	94
Low calorie mayonnaise	94
Low calorie blue cheese dressing	95

ESSENTIAL
LOW CALORIE TREATS

It's true – you can go on a diet and still eat your favourite foods. With some adjustments to cooking methods and ingredients it is possible to lose weight while eating your favourite meals. Roast potatoes, pies, cakes, Lancashire hot pot, chocolate ice cream – these are but a few of the recipes which are guaranteed to change your attitude to dieting. This book explains how many of the recipes have been altered to reduce the calories while retaining the taste. Compare the recipes in this book with your own recipes for the same meals and you will soon see how to adjust the ingredients and cooking methods for other dishes.

If you have just finished a diet and want to keep your weight down or you are just starting a diet and want some ideas for delicious low calorie meals the answers are here.

Whether your family is overweight or you just want to protect their health and future by helping them to eat properly, this book is full of low calorie treats to help you.

Start with breakfast – the most fattening things we eat in the morning are fried bacon, fried eggs, fried bread and toast loaded with butter.

Try changing to this breakfast and see if your family enjoy it. Buy *lean* back or streaky bacon and *grill it on a rack*. Don't keep the bacon fat. Toast the bread while you poach the eggs. An egg coddler is ideal for this as you can cook more than one at a time. If you don't have one then poach the eggs one by one in a small saucepan of lightly salted boiling water with a tea-spoon of vinegar. As the water boils stir the water fast so that it makes a whirlpool. Tip the egg into the whirlpool and keep stirring gently until cooked. Keep the cooked eggs warm until the rest are ready. Cut each slice of toast in half and place on a warm plate. Place an egg on top and the rashers of bacon by the side. Put salt and black pepper on the egg and it's ready to eat.

Do not butter the toast, use low fat spread – if you wish you can heat up some frozen chopped spinach and pour this onto the toast with the egg on top

Easy muesli
This will keep well in an airtight jar
2 cups rye flakes
2 cups porridge oats
1 cup oat bran
2 cups barley flakes
1 cup sultanas
1 cup dried banana and seedless raisins
Mix together and serve with semi-skimmed or skimmed milk or, better still, soak in fruit juice. *Apple juice will make it sweet without adding any sugar.*
Try adding a spoonful of very low fat fruit or plain yoghurt on the top and you have a breakfast with far fewer calories than usual.

Granola
This is ideal for sprinkling on low fat yogurt or even mixing in with your muesli
You can increase the amount of dried fruits to make a snack or something to nibble on a journey. Granola keeps well in airtight jars so it is worth making a big jar full.
500g instant rolled oats - preferably a mixture of medium and jumbo size
1 tablespoon rapeseed oil

2 tablespoons honey
250g mixed dried fruit (sultanas, raisins,
currants)
A wok is ideal for making this - otherwise
use a large non-stick pan. Heat the oil and
honey together in the bottom of the pan,
throw in the oats and toss constantly until
they are coated with the honey and oil
mixture and start to turn a golden brown.
Add the mixed fruit and continue to toss
for about a minute. Remove from heat and
toss from time to time as the mixtue cools.
When cold pack into jars.

For a delicious breakfast just add a little
skimmed milk and a fresh diced apple or
other fresh fruit and/or a natural yoghurt.
Try with an heaped tablespoon of
wheatgerm per bowl.
*This also makes a meal-in-a-plate for any time
of day.*

Starters and salads
Prawn Cocktail
serves 4

Many people believe the prawns are the fattening part of this dish – not so, usually it is the mayonnaise. Make it with a virtually fat free seafood dressing and many calories vanish.

400g cooked peeled prawns
4-5 crisp green lettuce leaves, shredded
1 untreated lemon
a few washed grapes, preferably black

For the dressing:
6 tablespoons low fat plain yoghurt
1 teaspoon mustard powder
½ teaspoon worcestershire sauce
½ teaspoon lemon juice
1 tablespoon of tomato ketchup
Cayenne pepper

Mix the dressing, adding cayenne pepper and salt to taste. Place the lettuce in four bowls with the prawns and grapes *(seeded & halved)* on top. Pour over the dressing and decorate with a thin slice of lemon.

Italian bean and tuna salad
serves 4-5 main, or 2 for a light meal
This Italian starter often contains a lot of oil but is easy to make with none at all. This greatly reduces the calories.

1 tin tuna in brine 200g
1 tin of butter beans 430g
½ small onion, thinly sliced
Lemon juice to taste
Freshly milled black pepper
2 teaspoons grated fresh ginger root
red pepper finely chopped
Drain the brine from tuna, and half the liquid from the beans, break up chunks of tuna with a fork and mix in with the beans. Add onion, pepper and lemon juice to taste and ginger and red pepper if you wish.

Garlic mushrooms
Visions of mushrooms covered in parsley and dripping in butter? Cook your mushroom this way and they will taste better and be virtually fat free. The secret here is 'sweating', this entails cooking in a heavy pan with only enough oil to prevent the food sticking.

2-3 large mushrooms per person
1 teaspoon olive oil
1 clove crushed garlic per person
1 tablespoon chopped parsley per person
freshly milled black pepper

Heat oil in a large lidded frying pan, add some of the garlic and turn the heat down low. Add mushrooms underside up with stems trimmed, sprinkle with the rest of the garlic. Cook over a low heat with the lid on to prevent steam escaping, this way the mushrooms cook in their own juices and taste delicious. Turn them once. When cooked sprinkle with parsley and serve. You can accompany the mushrooms with a little unbuttered toast to mop up the mushroom juices.

Waldorf salad   *serves 4*
The only thing to change in this traditional salad is the mayonnaise, the low calorie version recommended here means you can swamp it in mayonnaise and still end up with a low calorie Waldorf salad.

250g diced, cooked, skinned, chicken (optional)
6 stalks of celery, 6 red apples
50g roughly chopped walnuts

1 iceburg lettuce
Low calorie mayonnaise *(see recipe)*
Juice of ½ lemon
Peel, core, and dice the apples and toss in
the lemon juice to prevent discolouring.
Slice the celery into thin slices and add to
the apple with the walnuts and chicken.
Gently stir in the mayonnaise. Shred the
lettuce and put in a large bowl, place apple
mixture on top. Chill for a while before
serving.
*With some good brown bread this makes a
delicious summer lunch.*

Tuna salad

*Tuna in brine has far less calories than tuna in
oil. This salad is good by itself served on a pile
of shredded lettuce or as a filling for a sandwich.
Use the tuna tin as a measure.*
1 medium tin tuna in brine
1 measure diced fennel *or* celery
½ measure finely diced cucumber, without
seeds or skin
1 tablespoon fresh chives, chopped
1 tablespoon low calorie dressing or
mayonnaise*(see recipes)*
1 medium tomato peeled, seeded & diced
Freshly ground pepper

Drain the brine from the tuna and roughly chop the fish. Add the celery, cucumber, dressing, chives and pepper. Garnish with tomato.

Chicken and potato salad   serves 2
1 cup cold skinned breast of chicken, diced
2 cups cooked potatoes peeled and diced
½ cup finely chopped red pepper
1 small pot low fat yoghurt
1 teaspoon cider *or* white wine vinegar
1 teaspoon olive oil
salt and freshly ground black pepper
Put the vinegar and some salt and pepper in a small bowl. Then add the oil and beat together. Add the yoghurt slowly stirring all the time and check for seasoning. Mix all ingredients together and serve on a bed of finely shredded lettuce
By mixing the oil and vinegar first you have your base for a vinaigrette. Then add the yoghurt slowly and you will keep the texture. It is much lower fat than mayonnaise and much lower calorie. Everyone will ask for more!

Potato salad   serves 4
500g potatoes, washed
3 sticks celery, finey sliced

2 tablespoons capers or finely sliced gerkins
2 tablespoons finely chopped parsley
1-2 apples, skinned, cored & finely chopped
Boil potatoes without peeling them. They must be barely cooked or they will fall to pieces in the salad. When cooked run under cold water and let them cool. Chop into bite-sized pieces. Mix the celery, apple, and capers in a bowl.

To make the mayonnaise:
125ml low fat plain yoghurt
123ml 0% fat creme fraiche
1 teaspoon wine vinegar
black pepper and salt
Mix the vinegar, mustard and seasoning together first, then slowly add the yoghurt and creme fraiche stirring all the time.

Add the parsley to the mayonnaise, then add the potatoes to the other ingredients and finally mix in the mayonnaise. Do not stir any more than necessary as the pieces of potato tend to break. Leave the salad a few hours in the fridge before eating.

Add corn niblets, frozen peas or pieces of lean ham to make this a meal in itself.

PASTA DISHES

The most fattening thing about pasta is usually the sauce, often loaded with cream or olive oil it can be very high in calories. Here are some tempting lower calorie alternatives.

Spaghetti bolognaise   serves 8

600g spaghetti
500g best quality lean mined meat
2 medium carrots cleaned & finely chopped
1-2 stalks celery (*remove strings*) chopped
1 large tin peeled Italian tomatoes
1-2 tablespoons tomato concentrate
1 bouquet garni
1 teaspoon sugar
1 teaspoon salt
freshly ground black peper
3-4 cloves garlic finely chopped
1 teaspoon olive oil or sunflower oil

Take a wide heavy bottomed casserole or frying pan. Little by little brown the meat in half the oil and put to one side. Pour away the fat that the mince produces. Sweat the diced vegetables in the rest of the oil. Add the meat and the rest of the ingredients. Cook on a brisk heat for ½ hour. Remove bouqet garni. Meanwhile cook spaghetti and serve piping hot.

Serve on risotto, any sort of pasta or as a snack

on a piece of plain wholemeal toast. This is a
good sauce to freeze in small containers and
bring out when you don't really feel like cooking. When thawed, taste the sauce and add any
extra seasoning if necessary.

Pasta spirals with mushroom sauce

serves 4

300g plain green pasta spirals
250g button mushrooms
1 clove garlic, crushed
1 teaspoon olive oil
400g ripe tomatoes
Black pepper
Fresh or dried oregano
Boil the water for the pasta while you make

17

the sauce and cook according to packet instructions. Chop the mushrooms into small pieces, sweat them in oil. When they are soft add the garlic, black pepper and oregano. Chop the tomatoes, add to the rest and stir over a low heat for a few minutes before adding to pasta.

Make this sauce in advance, then make some thin pancakes using semi skimmed milk, stuff with the sauce and reheat in the oven when it is time to eat. Serve with salad or green vegetables. The whole family love this pancake dish.

Carbonara sauce for your favourite pasta
serves 4

Normally a sauce to avoid because of all the cream, here is the low calorie version.

300g pasta, cooked
200ml very low fat creme fraiche
100g lean ham, all visible fat trimmed off
freshly milled black pepper and salt
1 clove garlic crushed

Put the garlic in a non-stick pan and stir over a low heat for 1 minute. Add the ham and keep them moving in the pan for 2-3 minutes. If much fat or water comes off the ham tip it out. Then add the creme fraiche and warm gently. *Do not overheat.* Add

seasoning and pour over pasta.
*A few finely chopped button mushrooms added
to the garlic make this even more delicious.*

Pasta with basil and tomatoes   serves 4
500g any green pasta
4 large tomatoes *or* 380g tin tomatoes
4 dessertspoons finely chopped fresh basil
1 teaspoon olive oil
1-2 cloves fresh garlic, crushed
Boil pasta in plenty of salted water. Put
olive oil and garlic in a pan and add the
tomatoes finely chopped. Heat through
and pour over the pasta. Mix in the fresh
basil.
This can be eaten hot or as a refreshing cold dish

Veal and mushroom sauce for pasta or rice
serves 4
150-200g escalope of veal beaten flat and
thin, trimmed of any sinew or fat
1 slice parma ham stripped of fat
200g button mushrooms
1 pot natural low fat yoghurt or 0% fat
fromage blance *(optional)*
3 tablespoons fresh tarragon finely chopped
½ chicken cube in 2 tablespoons boiling
water

1 teaspoon oil

Finely slice the veal and ham into match stick strips. Clean and finely slice the mushrooms into slivers and put into a non-stick saute pan or wok over a medium heat. Toss them constantly, they will lose some water as they cook. When the water stops evaportaing add the oil and pieces of meat stirring all the time. The meat will also give off liquid. This should take about 5 minutes. Add the stock, stir thoroughly. Reduce heat, stir in yoghurt and parsley. Add freshly ground black pepper.

You can prepare this sauce in advance and gently reheat .

Green tagliatelli with chicken   *serves 4*

500g green tagliatelle, cooked
2 cups diced cooked chicken
2 cups chopped peeled *(or tinned)* tomato
1 tablespoon finely chopped dill *or* tarragon
1 tablespoon dry white wine
freshly ground black pepper and salt

Combine the above ingredients and stir into the pasta when it has been drained and still piping hot. Serve immediately.

Soups and light meals

Cream of tomato soup   *serves 6*

2 large tins peeled plum tomatoes
750ml chicken *or* vegetable stock
1 small onion finely chopped
freshly milled black pepper
125ml pot very low fat creme fraiche
1 teaspoon brown sugar
1 tablespoon chopped, fresh parley or basil
Cook onion in a little stock until soft. Finely chop tomatoes and add pepper and sugar with rest of stock. Bring to the boil. Liquidise and add the parsley or basil. When the soup is smooth, reheat – *do not let it boil.* Stir in the creme fraiche just before serving.

Vichyssoise   *serves 4*

3 medium leeks, trimmed of all green
1 small onion

200g peeled potato
600ml degreased chicken or vegetable stock
freshly ground black pepper, salt
freshly grated nutmeg
150ml very low fat creme fraiche
1 teaspoon sunflower oil
2 tablespoons chopped chives *or* spring onions
Slice leeks, potato and onion into thin strips. Sweat in a thick pan until leeks and onions are soft. *Do not let the onions brown.* Add the stock and season. Cover and simmer for 20 minutes. Cool and blend. Stir in the creme fraiche, leaving a swirl on the top. Chill in the fridge for at least 12 hours and serve with chives or spring onions sprinkled over.

Leek and potato soup with mussels

serves 4

This is a tasty alternative to mussels cooked in cream and white wine.
To cook the soup:
1 kg potatoes
750g trimmed leeks
1 large onion
1 tablespoon dijon mustard
1 teaspoon olive oil
degreased chicken stock, dry cider

Finely chop onion, cook until soft in olive oil. Add sliced leeks and potatoes cut into small cubes. Add chicken stock to half cover vegetables, then just cover them with the cider, add mustard and black pepper. Do not add salt if using a stock cube. Cook until potatoes are ready, the longer it cooks the better it gets. If you need more liquid during the cooking add water.

To cook the mussels:
8 well cleaned, sorted mussels per person
dry cider
a large cooking pot
Heat 2 inches of cider in the bottom of your pot. Add mussels, and put the lid on, they will cook in the steam. They are ready when shells open. Discard any unopened mussels. Serve soup in large bowls with mussels on top.

Minestrone
1 small onion, finely chopped
1 clove garlic, crushed
1 teaspoon olive oil
380g tin peeled plum tomatoes, chopped
2 sticks celery finely chopped
½ teaspoon dried oregano
1 bayleaf, pinch of died rosemary

2 teaspoons chopped, fresh basil
2 tablespoons tomato concentrate
salt and freshly milled black pepper
2 medium carrots
½ green pepper finely diced
850ml vegetable stock
25g vermicelli
1 tablespoon chopped fresh parsley
Put oil, onion, celery and garlic in bottom of a thick pan. Cover and sweat over a low heat for 5 minutes. Then add other ingredients except vermicelli and parsley. Simmer for half an hour then add the vermicelli and simmer until cooked. Add parsley just before serving.

Cream of pumpkin soup   *serves 4*
750g firm orange pumpkin, peeled & diced
1 medium onion, peeled & finely chopped
800ml light chicken stock
stalks and leaves of 1 bunch parsley
2 teaspoons tomato concentrate
1 sprinkle cayenne pepper *(optional)*
salt and plenty freshly ground pepper
1 small pot low fat creme fraiche *or* 300ml low fat milk with 2 teaspoons cornflour
2 teaspoons cooking oil
In a heavy stew pan or soup pot sweat the

onions and pumpkin pieces for 8-10 minutes. Add the stock, parsley stalks, tomato concentrate and seasonings and bring to the boil. Simmer gently for about 30 minutes. Remove parsley stalks, cool and blend little by little. Return to the pan and add the creme or milk. Gently reheat.

Clam chowder   serves 6 'meal-in-a-plate'
2 tins prepared clams *or* 1 packet frozen clams *or* 2 pints fresh clams *(just wash shells, discarding any that are broken or open and place in a wide pan over a brisk heat. When they open remove from shells, sieve the juice they give off and keep to add to the chowder)*
2 rashers thick cut back bacon with fat removed, diced
1 large onion, finely chopped
4 small carrots, diced
4 small potatoes, diced
1-2 cloves juicy garlic finely chopped
1 large tin *(750g)* peeled tomatoes drained and roughly chopped
A bouquet garni
freshly ground black pepper and salt
1 tablespoon oil
1 glass red wine
Chop the clams. In a large heavy casserole

sweat the onions, potatoes and carrots.
Cover with water add the bouquet garni
and cook on medium heat until just cooked.
Add the chopped clams, their juices, the
garlic and tomatoes. Cook for 10-15 minutes, season and serve.

*If you prefer creamy chowder omit the tomatoes
and when the chowder is piping hot and ready
to serve remove from the heat and stir in 1 small
pot of low fat creme fraiche. Serve with hot
french bread or a slice of wholemeal bread and
a glass of full red wine.*

Cream of chicken soup   serves 4
1.5 litres degreased chicken stock
6 tablespoons cooked diced chicken
1 teaspoóns fresh lemon juice
freshly milled black pepper and salt
6 tablespoons very low fat creme fraiche
1½ tablespoons sunflower oil
1 tablespoon plain white flour
a little paprika to garnish
First make a roux by heating the oil in a pan
and stirring in the flour. Keep stirring all
the time while you add the chicken stock
little by little. Do not rush this part and stir
out any lumps in between additions of
stock. Add the lemon juice, salt and pep-

per. Simmer for 25 minutes. Add the creme fraiche and chicken. Heat through – do not let the soup boil. Serve with a little paprika on each bowl.

Tomato and onion tart   *serves 2*
Make a low calorie pastry *(see recipe)* roll it out and put in a 20cm tart tin lined with greaseproof paper.
1 large onion, finely chopped
1 teaspoon olive oil
1 clove garlic, very finely chopped
500g ripe tomatoes, peeled, seeded, and chopped or tinned peeled plum tomatoes
1 teaspoon mixed thyme and rosemary, finely chopped *(or1 teaspoon dried oregano)*
Salt and freshly ground pepper
2 tablespoons grated parmesan cheese
100g grated gruyere cheese
50g finely slice mozarella cheese
8 pitted black olives halved
Sweat the onion in the heated olive oil. While it begins to soften add the garlic. Cook for 2 minutes, add the tomatoes, herbs, and seasoning and turn the heat up to reduce the sauce. Sprinkle the parmesan and gruyere over the pastry base, then spread the tomato on top. Finally cut some

very thin onion rings and arrange these over the top too. Cook in a preheated oven 180C for 40 minutes

Stir fry with rice   serves 4
200g sliced button mushrooms
12 oz beansprouts fresh
200g shredded white cabbage
1 teaspoon oil
½ cup vegetable stock
400g diced chicken breast *or* monkfish
2 tablespoons soy sauce
Juice of ½ lemon
1 tablespoon white wine vinegar
In a large pan or wok boil the cabbage in the stock until it evaporates then add oil, mushrooms and chicken or monkfish. Stir fry until cooked, 2-3 minutes, and add the beansprouts. Add salt and black pepper. Serve with brown or white rice.
If you want to make this in large quanities it is better to cook in batches so you do not lower the temperature of the oil too much.

Cheese omelette
The 1 egg omelette
One egg makes a good omelette and is possible in any pan though a good omelette

pan is always better. Beat your egg to an even consistency with some salt and pepper and a tablespoon of water. The water makes the omelette light and fluffy. Do not add milk. Heat 1 teaspoon or less of oil or butter in the pan and when hot add the egg mixture. When the edges of the omelette are getting firm pull them to the centre with a wooden spoon. Make one omelette per person, fold over and keep warm in the oven. Use soft cheese in place of cheddar as it is lower in fat. Try brie or camembert diced onto the omelette. Another low fat alternative is cottage cheese with black pepper and slivers of spring onion. Served with a green salad and a piece of toast this is a good light meal.

For a tasty change, make your 1 egg omelette. Carefully lay it flat on a board and spread cooked shredded spinach over the omelette. Roll it up like a swiss roll and let it cool. Slice then rounds of omelette and spinach spirals and serve as a starter – 1 omelette for 2 people.

Rissotto   serves 4

250g round rice
2 tablespoons chopped shallots or onion
1 clove finely chopped garlic
2 tablespoons dry white wine
2 tablespoons low fat creme fraiche
freshly ground black pepper and salt
1 chicken cube in a pint boiling water
more boiling water on hand.

Sweat the onions and garlic in the oil in a heavy deepish pan. Put the rice in a strainer and wash it quickly under running cold water. Add it to the onions and sweat, stirring all the time for about a minute. Pour on the hot stock little by little so that the liquid does not stop boiling. Stir to prevent sticking. When the rice has absorbed all the stock add the white wine, pepper and salt. Taste. If it is not cooked add the boiling water little by little until it is just soft. Stir in the creme fraiche, cover and leave for 5 minutes before serving. You can add a handful of fresh herbs finely chopped, chopped lean ham, prawns or a cup of cooked chicken to make this a meal in itself.

Children usually love this so make plenty. It is a good mixture for making into rice cakes and baking in the oven. Add a beaten egg to bind it together.

Kedgeree　　　　　　　　　　　serves 6
250g smoked haddock fillet
250g smoked herring fillet
250g any white fish fillet steamed
275g long grain rice
pinch of saffron or ½ teaspoon turmeric
150g button mushrooms, cut in quarters
1 onion, finely chopped
2 tablespoons finely chopped fresh parsley
300ml skimmed milk
2 teaspoons lemon juice
1 heaped teaspoon strong curry powder
cayenne pepper
1 teaspoon olive oil
125ml very low fat creme fraiche
Cut the fish into bite sized pieces. Place the

herring in ½ the milk and leave for ½ hour.
Then put in a saucepan and bring to the
boil, simmer for 5 minutes. Put the haddock in the other half of the milk, bring to
the boil and simmer for 5-10 minutes. Discard the milk from the herring. Preheat
your oven to 180C. Sweat the onions and
mushrooms in the olive oil in a pan with a
lid on. Cook the rice with the saffron in the
water. When the rice is nearly cooked stir
in the curry powder and cayenne pepper
and lemon juice. When cooked transfer the
rice to an ovenproof casserole, fold in the
fish and the milk from the haddock, then
stir in the creme fraiche. Put the mushrooms and onions on top and place in the
oven for 30 minutes with a lid on. Sprinkle
fresh parsley over the top before serving.

Meat dishes
Coq au vin   *serves 2*
2 chicken quarters, skinned
4 shallots, peeled
2 cloves garlic finely chopped
4 carrots sliced in thin rounds
1 teaspoon olive oil
600ml dry red wine
freshly ground black pepper

200g button mushrooms, sliced
Sweat the mushrooms and garlic with the olive oil in a thick bottomed oven proof dish with a lid on. Add the chicken, shallots and carrots. Pour over the red wine and add water if necessary to bring the level of liquid to half cover the chicken. Add seasoning. Cook in preheated oven 190C for 1 hour. Serve with rice or mashed potatoes and a green vegetable.

Moroccan spicy chicken   *serves 4*
4 chicken quarters, skinned
4 spanish onions
450g tomatoes, skinned & seeded *or* tinned
2 sticks of cinnamon *or* 1 teaspoon powder
2 tablespoons olive oil
Large pinch saffron in 50ml boiling water
½ teaspoon ground ginger
3 tablespoons fresh chopped parsley
½ teaspoon salt
½ teaspoon freshly milled black pepper
You need a heavy casserole with a lid. Preheat oven to 175C, slice 2 of the onions and chop up the other 2. Cut tomatoes into large chunks. Put 1 teaspoon oil in the bottom of the casserole, then the chicken and cinnamon., Cover the chicken with a

layer of sliced onions, then tomatoes. Mix all the other ingredients and pour over. Cover the casserole and place in the oven for 1½ hours, a little less if your chicken pieces are small. This dish can be eaten hot or cold with rice or potatoes and green beans.

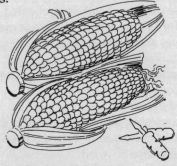

Chicken and corn casserole   serves 4-5
Very quick to make, reheats well.
3 large *or* 4 medium breasts chicken cut into bite sized chunks
1 teaspoon oil
2 tins corn in brine
3 tomatoes peeled, seeded and chopped
1 large onion, finely sliced
a bunch fresh parsley, finely chopped
2 cloves garlic
½ chicken cube in ½ a pint boiling water

1 small carton low fat creme fraiche
freshly ground black pepper and salt
a little cayenne pepper
To start this off use a wok or a skillet and
toss the chicken pieces and onion with the
oil to seal the meat. Put on the lid and
sweat for 5 minutes making sure nothing
sticks or burns. Transfer to an ovenproof
dish, add drained corn and tomatoes and
heat in a medium oven for about 15 minutes – it must not dry out. When ready to
serve stir in the creme fraiche and serve
with hot baps or warm pitta bread.

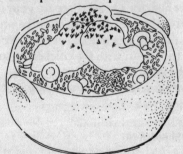

Chicken with peppers and rice   serves 4
1 chicken 1.5 kg, cut into quarters
2 large green peppers, halved and deseeded
1kg tomatoes, peeled, deseeded and cut
into chunks

2 onions, diced
3 cloves garlic, finely chopped
1 teaspoon sweet paprika
freshly milled black pepper
salt
2 teaspoons olive oil
200g rice

In a heavy pan with a lid heat the olive oil and brown the chicken pieces, remove the chicken from the pan and put on one side. Turn the heat down and gently cook the onions. Add the peppers, tomatoes and garlic. Season to taste. Cover and cook on a low heat for 1 hour. Prepare your rice in the usual way. Add the paprika and stir into the rice just before serving. You can mix the rice in with the chicken or serve it on the side.

Paprika loses its taste very quickly, make sure yours is fresh.

Roast chicken

Find a chicken without much fat evident. It is best to roast chicken with skin intact and remove later.

Cut into quarters 1 apple, 1 untreated lemon and 1 small onion and stuff chicken with these. Roast chicken on spit if possible, if

not, roast in preheated oven 180C for 1 hour or longer. Make gravy with gravy powder – *not fat from chicken.*
Eat with peas, new potatoes rolled in low fat plain yoghurt and finely chopped fresh parsley. Try carrots with a little powdered ginger instead of butter.

Chicken livers

This can be served with risotto, pasta or creamed potatoes or blended and used as a spread on toast or cracker biscuits.

250g chicken livers
Freshly ground black pepper
Salt
2 heaped tablespoons chopped parsley
2 tablespoons brandy *or* whisky
1 pot (20cl) low fat creme fraiche *(if used as a spread)*
1 tablespoon onion, finely chopped
1 clove garlic, finely chopped
2 tablespoons oil
You need a heavy skillet or non-stick frying pan. Clean and roughly chop the chicken livers. Put them with the oil, garlic and onions into the pan and cook until each piece is just pale pink in the centre. Add the alcohol and bring to the boil. Stir, taste and

season, then add the parsley.

If you want to use the chicken livers as a pate or spread add the cream and blend for a minute. Pile into a small serving dish and refrigerate.

Kidney and mushroom skewers

Allow 2 or 2½ kidneys per person. Have the butcher peel them and open them out flat removing the grissle. Thread onto skewers and cook under a fairly fierce grill, they should be faintly pink in the centre. Overcooked they become tough and dry. Serve with a dish of large garlic mushrooms and wholegrain or rice with plenty of freshly chopped parsley added.

Chicken with cider   *serves 2*

2 boned skinned chicken breasts *or* 4 drumsticks
Dry cider
8 prunes
1 large cooking apple
4 oz mushrooms chopped
1 teaspoon oil
Salt, pepper

Put oil in thick casserole. Sweat onion, seal chicken, turning a couple of times in the oil on high heat. Remove chicken from pot.

Add mushrooms and cook on low heat with lid on until soft. Add chicken, apples and enough cider to just cover. Add prunes, season to taste. Cook in preheated oven 180C for 40 minutes with lid on. Then turn oven to low for 1 hour to thicken sauce. Serve with peas, brown bread or new potatoes.

Roast turkey

This is a faster way of cooking the Christmas turkey and does not require constant basting.
For a 4kg turkey:
Stuff the turkey your usual way and wrap the bird in tinfoil, making sure that it is tightly sealed. Place in preheated oven 220C and cook for 2½ hours. Remove foil and cook for a further 20-30 minutes until the skin is brown and crispy. Tip away any fat from the bird and make gravy with gravy powder. Don't eat the skin.

Roast beef   *serves 6*

The secret to a low fat roast is to get on well with your butcher and ask him to trim the roast well and sell you the leanest cut. Leave some fat around the joint for roasting but trim this off when you carve.

2kg joint sirloin on the bone
Salt & pepper
2 cloves garlic *(optional)*

Rub the salt and pepper over the joint and leave in the fridge overnight. cut the garlic into quarters, make small holes in the joint with a very sharp knife and push in the garlic.   Roast the meat on a rack in a roasting pan in a preheated oven 220C for 1¼ hours for rare meat. Add another 20 minutes to the cooking time for well done. Serve with horseradish sauce, dry roasted potatoes and low calorie yorkshire pudding.

Make gravy with gravy powder and don't mop up all the dripping with a piece of bread!

Yorkshire pudding

This is traditionally cooked under the roasting meat so that all the fat drips on to the pudding. Obviously this is not going to lower the saturated fat content of your meal. This recipe uses olive oil instead of beef dripping and semi skimmed milk.

100g plain flour
1 egg
300ml semiskimmed milk *(not skimmed)*
salt
1 tablespoon olive oil
Sift the flour and salt into a mixing bowl, add the egg into a dip in the flour. Pour in some of the milk and gently stir the flour into the milk a little at a time. Keep adding the milk and stirring in the flour. When it is all mixed beat the batter until you see plenty of bubbles in it. Cover and leave to settle for 20 minutes. Put the oil in the baking tin and heat until it begins to smoke a little. Remove from the heat and pour in batter. Put the tin in the top of a preheated oven for 35 minutes. Leave a little longer if the pudding is not golden brown.

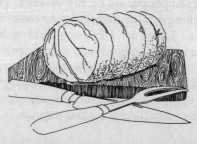

Lamb kebabs   *serves 4*

4-8 skewers to suit your grill

500g lean lamb, preferably from the leg

8-12 button mushrooms, wiped and trimmed

4 bayleaves, halved

1 red pepper seeded and cut into squares

8 small shallots

1 teaspoon dried rosemary

1 clove garlic, crushed or finely chopped

Juice of small lemon

Salt & freshly ground black pepper

1 teaspoon olive oil

250ml natural low fat yoghurt

Fresh mint *(this is very important)*

1-2 hours before serving make a marinade
by mixing the oil, lemon juice, rosemary,
pepper, salt and garlic together in a bowl.
Dice the meat *(fairly large pieces as it is not
good if too cooked)*. Thread the skewers so
that meat, mushrooms, bayleaves, shallots
and red pepper are evenly divided. Place
in a long serving dish and pour over marinade. Leave for 1-2 hours turning from
time to time. When ready to cook, preheat
grill and place the skewers on the rack,
turn constantly. *Serve with a bowl of yoghurt
and fresh finely chopped mint leaves and plenty
of rice, pitta bread or mashed potatoes.*

Guinea fowl with prunes serves 4
A rich dish for a special occasion

1 guinea fowl weighing about 1.5kg trussed and cleaned

1 medium onion

12 large fat prunes soaked in tea overnight

2 teaspoons 0% fat fromage blanc

2 glasses good red wine

Bouqet garni

freshly ground black pepper, salt

water or stock if necessary

Put the onion cut into quarters with the fromage blanc into the cavity of the bird, this keeps it moist, and paint the oil over the breast and legs. In a heavy casserole, brown the bird quickly over a high heat. Pour on the wine and when it comes to the boil lower the heat. Add the pepper and salt and put in a pre-heated oven (175C) with a lid on and leave for 20 minutes. Drain the prunes and add to the pan. If the wine has evaporated add a little water or light stock, baste the bird with the juices, cover and return to the oven. Cook slowly for another 40-60 minutes. Carve and pour over the juices from the pan. Serve with mashed potato and celeriac and a green vegetable like broccoli or french beans.

This dish can be made very successfully with pheasant. In general, game contains less fat than pork, beef, and lamb.

Rabbit with green peppers   serves 4
1 medium rabbit, jointed
1 tablespoon oil
2 glasses white wine
Bunch parsley
2 tablespoons finely chopped shallots
1 green pepper seeded and sliced in rounds
1 chicken cube in 1 pint boiling water
1 clove garlic, finely chopped
freshly ground pepper, salt
½ cup 0% fat fromage blanc
Seal the pieces of rabbit with the oil in the

bottom of a heavy ovenproof casserole.
Just cover with the stock and wine and
cook for 20 minutes in a medium oven.
Add the onion, garlic and pepper rings and
cook for a further 20 minutes turning the
pieces of meat over so that they do not dry
out. Just before serving stir in the fromage
blanc and garnish with the parsley. Serve
straight from the dish with creamed or
new potatoes.
*Rabbit generally contains very little fat and is
very tasty. Look out for rabbit recipes or ask
your butcher for advice.*

Low fat steak and kidney pie   serves 6
*This is a version of a traditional recipe with the
fat content considerably reduced. There is less
pastry than some recipes which have a pie base
and top, and the pasty used is low fat.*
750g boneless neck of beef with fat trimmed
1 ox kidney
1 large onion, finely chopped
1 teaspoon sunflower oil
250ml plain flour
salt and freshly ground black pepper
1 bayleaf
2 tablespoons chopped parsley
low calorie pastry

Clean the kidney by soaking in warm salted water for a few minutes then cut in half, remove the hard centre and the outer membrane. Cut into small cubes and the beef into bite-sized cubes. Brown these in preheated sunflower oil, add the onion and when this is transparent, the seasoning. Add the heated stock to the meat, cover and simmer for 2 hours or until meat is tender. If necessary thicken the liquid with a little flour. When the meat has cooled slightly put in a pie dish with a pie funnel or upturned egg cup. Roll out the pastry over the funnel to allow steam to escape. Brush with skimmed milk and bake in preheated oven at 200C for 20 minutes or until the pastry is cooked.
Serve with loads of green vegetables or crispy green salad

Lancashire hot pot serves 4

Lamb can be a fatty meat but there are ways of reducing the amount of fat in this traditional British dish while retaining the taste. You need to make it at least 8 hours before you want to eat.
500g leanest lamb, with all visible fat trimmed, cut into bite-sizes chunks
600g potatoes in thick slices

150g mushrooms thickly sliced
2 lambs kidneys skinned and sliced with
the membranes removed
1 large onion, finely chopped
1 clove garlic, crushed *(optional)*
Small branch fresh thyme
Freshly ground black pepper and salt
300ml degreased beef *or* vegetable stock
You will need half the potatoes when you
make this and the rest when you reheat it.
Put a layer of potatoes in the bottom of an
ovenproof casserole. Sprinkle a little salt
and pepper over these and then cover with
the mushrooms. Arrange lamb, kidneys
and onion on top. Pour over the stock with
the thyme. Cover and place in preheated
oven, 180C for 2¼ hours. Remove the casserole and cool for 8 hours. Remove the
thyme. A lot of fat will have solidfied on
the surface, remove this with a spoon and
paper towel. Do not stir. When you want
to eat, parboil the rest of the potato slices
and arrange them on the top of the meat.
Put the casserole back into a preheated
oven 200C and cook for 40 minutes. The
hot pot should be warmed through and the
potatoes golden brown. Traditionally this
dish does not have carrots in it but there is

no reason why you cannot put a layer of carrots under the meat and slightly increase the amount of stock if you want to make this dish go a little further.

Use thes ideas to reduce the fat next time you make any kind of lamb stew or casserole.

Hamburgers   serves 4

450g very lean minced meat
1 onion, very finely chopped
1 tablespoon tomato puree
2 tablespoons wholemeal breadcrumbs
1 clove garlic, crushed
freshly milled black pepper
1 egg
salt

Mix everything together and leave for an hour. Pat the meat into shape and cook under a hot grill or on a barbeque. Serve in a wholemeal bun with plenty of coleslaw, made from white cabbage and grated carrot in low fat yoghurt, a squeeze of lemon juice and freshly milled black pepper.

Pepper steaks   serves 4

This is steak with a cream sauce. By using low fat creme fraiche you not only get more flavour but also reduce the amount of fat and hence calories. It is important not to heat the sauce too much. Low fat alternatives are particularly likely to separate if overheated.

2 dessertspoons crushed black peppercorns
4 fillet steaks, all visible fat trimmed
2 dessertspoons brandy
1 teaspoon olive oil
4 tablespoons low fat creme fraiche

At least 20 minutes before you plan to cook them press two thirds of the pepper into the steaks on both sides. In a thick pan heat the oil. Sear the steaks on both sides until cooked as you like. Remove steaks and keep hot. Pour the brandy into the same pan and when hot set light to it. Lower the heat and when there is no more flame add the creme fraiche. Warm through, add a little salt and the rest of the pepper and pour some over each steak as you serve.

Rumpsteak with red wine sauce   *serves 2*
This is another alternative to a creamy sauce for your steak.
2 thick pieces best grilling steak, 250g each.
1 glass red wine
1 teaspoon oil
8-10 shallots
2 teaspoons dijon mustard
freshly ground black pepper and salt
Peel and finely slice the shallots, sweat them in the oil in a heavy bottom pan with a lid. When they are softened pour on the wine and bring to the boil. Reduce heat and simmer for about 5 minutes. Season with pepper and mustard. Taste and add salt if necessary. Grill the steak in the usual way and when done carve into inch wide strips. Pour over the sauce and serve with a puree of potatoes and celeriac or plain boiled potatoes and green beans.

Meatloaf a la wintle   *serves at least 6*
This is a low calorie version of a generally not very low calorie dish. Calories are lost here by using the leanest mince you can find and by using skimmed milk. If you have a non-stick meatloaf tin you need not oil it.
2 slices bread, crusts removed

3 tablespoons skimmed milk
500g lean mince beef
200g sausagemeat *(ask the butcher for one with less fat)*
1 small green pepper
2 onions
1-2 cloves garlic
pinch of mixed herbs
Seeds of 6 cardamon pods *(optional)*
1 tablespoon tomato puree
1 egg
6 rashers streaky bacon, rindless
4-5 bayleaves
Olive oil

Preheat oven to 200C. Put slices of bread in a shallow dish, pour over the milk and leave to soak. Mix the mince and the sausagemeat thoroughly. Finely chop the onions, garlic and pepper (remove the seeds) and mix in with the meat. Add the herbs, spices and tomato puree. Mix in the bread, beat the egg in the bread dish and add that last. If your meatloaf tin is not non-stick lightly grease with olive oil. Arrange the bayleaves in a pattern in the bottom of your tin. Lay the rashers of bacon across the bottom of the tin, they should reach up the sides a little way.

Spoon the meatloaf mixture into the tin, neaten it, any long bits of bacon fold over the top. Cover with tinfoil and press firmly into the tin. Cook in the oven for 1¼ hours. When cooked turn the meatloaf out on to a plate. The bayleaves should now be decorating the top.
Good hot or cold with jacket potatoes and a tomato and onion salad.
Dieters should not eat the bacon strips.

Beef strogonoff   serves 6
The cream in this recipe is replaced with low fat yoghurt which gives the sauce a nice sharp taste while still being creamy. The leaner the beef the fewer calories there will be.
500g lean grilling steak, cut into thin strips
2 teaspoons sunflower oil
2 large onions, sliced thinly
500g button mushrooms, sliced thinly
1 heaped teaspoon mustard powder
salt and freshly ground black pepper
2 teaspoons lemon juice
250ml degreased meat stock
250ml low fat yoghurt
Watercress *or* fresh parsley to garnish
Heat the oil in a thick bottomed pan, add the meat and brown quickly over a high

heat – *if you do not do this quickly the meat will get tough.* Remove the meat and put to one side. Add mushrooms and onions to the pan and turn the heat down very low. When the onions are translucent and the mushrooms soft, add the meat again and the pepper, salt, lemon juice and mustard. Heat the meat stock in a separate pan and pour over the meat. Cover with a lid and simmer for 20 minutes. Remove from heat and stir in the yoghurt.
Serve with new potatoes or rice.

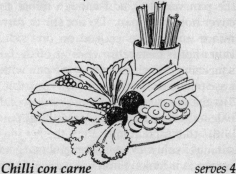

Chilli con carne   serves 4
450g lean minced beef
350g tin peeled plum tomatoes
1 large onion, finely chopped
1 tin red kidney beans, juice drained
2 cloves garlic, finely chopped

2-3 generous teaspoons chilli powder
2 tablespoons tomato puree
½ teaspoon dried oregano
½ teaspoon dried thyme
2 bayleaves
cayenne pepper and salt
1 beef stock cube in 250ml water

If you substitute the mince for soya mince and use 2 teaspoons of yeast extract or a vegetable stock cube this can be served as a vegetarian meal.

Seal the mince in a heavy frying pan, get the pan very hot, add enough mince to cover bottom of pan. Do not stir or turn mince until it has cooked on one side. When both sides are brown drain off the fat squeezing the mince against the pan with a spatula to drain as much fat as possible. Tip the fat away. Cook meat in several batches. When all ready place in large pan with other ingredients. Vary the hot seasoning to suit your taste. Remember it gets spicier as it cooks. Simmer for 45 minutes or longer to thicken sauce. Serve with rice and/or green salad.

You can buy taco shells in the supermarket and fill them with this chili mixture. You remove most of the fat from the mince with this cooking method, so if the leaner mince is more expensive don't worry you can still reduce the fat content of a less expensive mince.

Frank's shepherds pie   *serves 4*
Courtesy of Franke Wintle, author. 'The pie has evolved over the years and yours should too. You like sweetcorn? Well then add some sweetcorn. Vary the quantities too, if you feel like it.
750g the very best minced beef you can get
5-6 medium sized potatoes
1 onion
1 clove garlic
1 small bag frozen petit pois
6 cardamons
pinch thyme *(fresh is best)*
1 pinch each ground coriander and cumin
6 juniper berries
a pinch of your favourite herb or spice
1 teaspoon olive oil
Peel potatoes, chop onion and garlic into small pieces, take the seeds from the cardamoms, throw the husks away. Cook the potatoes and juniper berries in lightly salted water a for 20 minutes. Cook the peas and put to one side. You are not going to cook the mince all at once. Heat a heavy frying

pan with just enough oil to smear the surface. Take a few cardamom seeds and the other herbs and spices and put them into the hot oil for a minute. Add the garlic and meat. Cook, stirring until the meat is browned all over. Then tip pan to one side and pour off fat. With a slotted spoon transfer it to an oven proof dish. Repeat this with meat, herbs, spices, onion and garlic until all the mince is in the pie dish. This is the crucial part of the operation – *don't try to fry all your mince in one go.* Mix peas in with the meat mixture. Mash the potatoes and spread them on top. This dish can be made a day before. To cook preheat oven to 200C, cook for 45-60 minutes. *Serve with a salad, enjoy and improvise.*

Fondue   serves 2
This is really delicious. As in many oriental dishes it is the preparation that takes the most time.
A fondue pan and burner and 2 long forks or wooden skewers to cook the food.
Prepare in advance and keep in the fridge:
75g fillet steak, beaten flat and cut into small bite sized strips
1 skinless breast of chicken, sliced the same

way

4 jumbo prawns, peeled, cut into fine strips

1 pint very light chicken or vegetable stock

Small bunch fresh coriander finely chopped
(*the stalk can go into the stock*)

Some ready-cooked long grain white rice
(*each person has an individual bowl of warm
rice*)

Mushroom or soy sauce

When you are ready to eat put the hot stock into the fondue pan and light the burner. The stock should be just simmering. Arrange the raw meat and fish on each plate with a little freshly chopped coriander mixed with soy sauce. The pieces of beef will take a fraction longer than the chicken and the chicken a little longer than the prawns. Spear one thing at a time and cook in the simmering stock then dip in to the coriander and soy sauce and with a fork or chop sticks drop into the rice, prepare the next piece for cooking and eat the first bit with a little rice. By the time all the meat, rice and prawns are finished you will have perfectly delicious soup which you can pour into the empty rice bowls and drink. *This is an infinitely lower calorie fondue than the cheese and wine one you dip bread into. It is not recommended for children. If you like hot spicy dishes and you can find a shop selling Japanese food, buy a tube of Wasabi or horse-radish paste and mix a little of this with your soy sauce.*

Fish dishes
Herring with mustard sauce　　　serves 4
4 herrings
250ml semiskimmed milk
50g oatmeal seasoned with salt and pepper
1 tablespoon sunflower oil
Low calorie white sauce with 1 tablespoon dijon mustard
Debone the herrings. Coat them in oatmeal by first dipping them in the milk in a shallow bowl and then pressing them lightly into the oatmeal on a plate. Make sure both sides are well coated. Heat the oil in a pan and cook for 7-10 minutes on both sides. Pour a little warm mustard sauce on the plate next to each fish.
Serve with wedges of lemon and green beans.

Salmon with sorrel sauce　　　serves 2
Ask the fishmonger to fillet the salmon tail for you so you have two nice fillets of salmon.
You need enough liquid to barely cover the

fish, a container with lid or enough tin foil to make a loose sealed packet around the fish. A good poaching liquid is half dry wine, half water with a pinch of dried tarragon.

You can poach on top or in oven. If on top be sure the liquid only simmers. Set the oven at 180C. Cook for fillets for 10-15 minutes

For the sauce you need:

1 tablespoon fresh chopped sorrel per fillet
2 tablespoons low fat fromage frais
a little skimmed milk
Freshly ground black pepper, salt

Mix all these together and warm gently in a frying pan do not overheat. If you cannot find fresh sorrel you can use fresh or dried tarragon. Tarragon is a stronger flavour, so use less.

Fish pie
serves 4

225g skinned white fish fillets, e.g. cod
225g skinned smoked fish fillets, cod or haddock
450g mashed potato
250ml white sauce
25g low fat spread
25g plain flour
250ml semi skimmed milk

Put milk into a saucepan and add the flour and low fat spread. Slowly bring sauce to a boil and whisk by hand until sauce thickens. Add salt, pepper and a pinch of nutmeg. To make the pie preheat oven to 190C. Cut fish into small cubes and mix with peas. Place in ovenproof dish leaving room for the potato on top. Pour white sauce over the fish, spread mashed potato evenly on top. The potato should cover to the edge of dish to seal moisture in the pie. Bake for 40-45 minutes until the potato is golden.

Sweet and sour prawns with courgettes
serves 4

1kg courgettes
300g ready cooked prawns peeled
2 tablespoons wine vinegar

1 tablespoon brown sugar
1 teaspoon olive oil
2 tablespoons water
20g pine nuts
30g sultanas
1 large clove garlic, crushed
Salt and freshly milled black pepper
Cutt the courgettes into thin strips about 5
cm long. Sprinkle with 1 teaspoon salt and
leave for 1 hour. Rinse and pat dry. Cook
the garlic in the oil on a low heat for a
couple of minutes and then add the courgettes. Stir gently for 2 minutes, add sugar,
vinegar, water and sultanas. Simmer for
10 minutes. Add nuts and prawns and
simmer for 5 minutes. If it begins to dry out
add a little more water. *Serve with rice.*

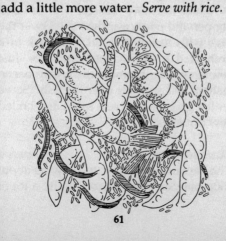

Baked cod   serves 4
4 fillets cod
½ teaspoon sunflower oil
Bayleaf and fresh thyme
2 tablespoons cornflour
4 thin rashers rindless streaky bacon grilled
until crispy
50g button mushrooms, thinly sliced
2 shallots finely sliced
Sweat the mushrooms and onions in the oil
until soft. Put these into an ovenproof dish
and stir in a teaspoon of fresh thyme leaves.
Lie the fish fillets over the mushrooms.
Heat the milk until nearly boiling and then
add the bayleaf. Stir the cornflour mixture
and bring to the boil. Keep stirring until
the sauce thickens. Season with salt and
pepper and pour over the fish. Cover the
dish with tinfoil or a lid and cook in a
preheated oven 220C for 10 minutes. Just
before serving crumble the crispy bacon
rashers and sprinkle over the fish. Serve
with a green watercress salad and boiled
new potatoes.

Skate with caper sauce   serves 4
Choose thick cuts of skate allowing about
250g per person as there is quite a lot of

waste. You need cold water to which you add ½ tablespoon white wine or cider vinegar, a sliced onion, a bayleaf, about 6 peppercorns and some parsley stalks if you have them. Bring the liquid to the boil and immediately reduce the heat so that the liquid is just barely trembling. Half cover and test after 20 minutes. Remove fish and drain then serve hot with hot new potatoes or creamed potatoes and the following sauce:

1 heaped tablespoon capers in vinegar
1 heaped tablespoon chopped parsley
½ tablespoon finely chopped onion
Fresh ground black pepper
20cl low fat creme fraiche
Few drops vinegar from caper jar if desired

This sauce can be served warm but it is very good served cold with the hot fish and potaotes.

This is a lower calorie alternative to the traditional skate in black butter and as delicious.

Baby squid in wine sauce   *serves 2*
Less calories than the deep fried version.
250g little squid about 5-10cm long
1 teaspoon olive oil

1 thick piece brown bread without crust
1 tablespoon finely chopped onion
1 clove garlic, crushed
1 glass red wine
Bunch fresh parsley, finely chopped
freshly ground black pepper and salt
Wash the squid under a running tap and
remove the hard transparent 'pen' from
the centre. Some people prefer to discard
the little head, the eyes, ink sacks and
tentacles but in fact all this is edible and
very good. The 'pen' which looks just like
a piece of plastic, is not. Use a pair of
kitchen scissors to chop the squids into
little rings and the heads into halves or
quarters. In a heavy skillet or frying pan
sweat the onion for 1 minute in the oil. Add
the pieces of squid. Stir them around over
a moderate heat for about 8 minutes. If
they cook too long they will become tough.
Crumble the brown bread and add to the
squid, then the wine and pepper and cook
for another 5-8 minutes over a slightly
brisker heat. Stir in the parsley and garlic.
Taste the sauce and add a little salt if
necessary. Serve on risotto or with bread.
*A variation on this dish which helps to spin it
out and weakens the rather strong flavour, is to*

*add peeled, chopped and seeded tomatoes, fresh
or tinned, at the same time as the wine.*

Sole with leeks   serves 2

2 fillets sole, 200g each
1 leek
1 stick celery
1 shallot
1 teaspoon lemon juice
1 teaspoon sunflower oil
20g plain flour, seasoned with salt
50ml dry white wine
3 tablespoons low fat creme fraiche
2 teaspoons fresh parsley chopped
4 slices untreated lemon

Dice the shallot, and the celery. Cut most
of the green part off the leeks and quarter
longways. Sweat these with the oil in a
heavy pan with a lid. When the leeks are
soft pour all the contents of the pan into an
ovenproof dish. Lightly coat the sole fillets
with the seasoned flour, roll them loosely
and nestle them into the vegetables. Pour
in the wine, cover and cook in a preheated
oven at 200C for 20 minutes. Remove from
the oven and pour the juice into original
heavy pan, add the creme fraiche, stir and
warm over a low heat. Pour over the fish

and return to the oven for 5 minutes. Garnish with the chopped parsley and slices of lemon and serve with new potatoes and spinach.

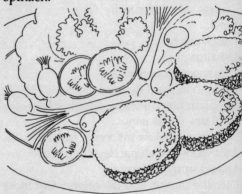

Fish cakes   *serves 4*
500g cod
400g mashed or creamed potatoes
salt and pepper
2 teaspoons horseradish sauce *(optional)*
2 tablespoons peas, cooked
1 egg white
1 teaspoon sunflower oil
Steam the cod and mash up with a fork. Mix in the potato, seasoning and egg white. Wash your hands thoroughly and pat the mixture into small cakes. If you have a

good non-stick frying pan use this, otherwise heat the teaspoon of oil in a frying pan and brown the fishcakes on both sides. *Serve with green beans, or broad beans and carrots.*

Sole with orange sauce and crepes serves 6
12 small fillets sole
Juice of three sweet oranges
Finely grated zest of 2 oranges
Parsley and very thin slices of orange to garnish
Batter
50g plain flour
Pinch of salt
1 egg
65 ml skimmed milk
4 tablespoons water
Make the batter early and leave it to rest for a while before making the pancakes. Sift flour and salt into a mixing bowl, lightly beat the egg and make a well in the centre of the flour to hold it. Mix together thoroughly then add the water and the milk slowly beating all the time until smooth. If it is too thick add a little more water. Lightly oil a thick frying pan with sunflower oil and make at least 4 pancakes

from the batter. Roll them up and cut slices to make rolled ribbons. Poach the sole in a large saucepan on top of the stove. Cover the fish completely with lightly salted water. Add a little parsley, a slice of onion, a few slices of carrot, one bayleaf, 5 peppercorns and 2 teaspoons of lemon juice. Bring to the boil and then cover and simmer until the fish flakes with a fork usually about 8 minutes depending on the size of the fillets. Remove the fish with a slotted spoon and place on a warm serving plate. Just before serving reheat the ribbons of pancake in the pan until golden, arrange with the cooked sole fillets. Heat the orange juice and zest with a couple of tablespoons of the poaching liquid and when just boiling pour over the fish and pancakes. Garnish with the parsley and orange slices.

Vegetables

Fat free roast potatoes   *serves 4*

My grandmother told me this was how she roasted potatoes during the war when fat and butter were hard to come by

500g peeled potatoes cut in ½ or in quarters
salt
large saucepan boiling water

Parboil the potatoes, drain well and pat dry. Place them in a baking tray, modern non-stick ones are ideal. Sprinkle the salt over the potatoes and place in a preheated oven 200C. Roast for 60-90 minutes depending on the size of potato.

If you cut the potato into approximately 3cm cubes before you parboil them you greatly cut down on cooking time and end up with delicious, tiny, fat free, roast potatoes.

69

Creamed potatoes
Allow one potato per person

Clean the potatoes, chop into roughly *'half an egg'* size pieces and steam. It is easy to invent a steamer but if you haven't one or can't improvise cook in as little water as possible starting with a lid on and boil until the water is used up. The potatoes should be soft when prodded with a fork. If you have a food mill, mouli your potatoes through the finest mesh. Then and then only you can season with pepper and salt adding a tablespoon of low fat creme fraiche. For a lower fat alternative you can use ½ tablespoon of 0% fat cottage cheese per person.

Nutty mashed potatoes

Prepare potatoes as recipe above for creamed potatoes. When the potatoes are cooked keep the skins on and mash with a potato masher then season and beat in low fat creme fraiche or cottage cheese with a fork. Potatoes cooked like this are delicious served with a meat stew or liver and onions.

Chips

Horror of horrors for serious dieters. The problem with chips is that they can absorb a lot of fat. To stop this they need to be cooked in very hot fat. This makes a crisp outer coating on a chip quickly so no more fat is absorbed. To do this you need to have a good groundnut or peanut oil to fry in and you need to cook your chips in small batches. This prevents the potatoes from lowering the temperature of the oil too much. Pat each batch of chips dry with paper towel to remove excess fat and keep warm in the oven.

Bought oven ready chips usually have a fairly low fat content.

Potato pancakes   *serves 4*
Mix together:

500g potatoes finely grated into a bowl (if you keep the skins on they'll add a nutty flavour)

1 large onion grated into the same bowl

2 heaped tablespoons plain flour

1 egg beaten separately in a small bowl

salt and freshly ground black pepper

2 teaspoons oil

Mix all the above except the oil together in

a large bowl. Cover the base and sides of
a heavy frying pan with half of the oil.
When it is hot pour in pancake mixture and
cook for about 8 minutes Slide on to a
plate. Repaint the frying pan with the
remaining oil and turn the uncooked side
of the pancake back into the hot pan. Press
down with a fish slice and cook until crisp
and golden.

Ratatouille   *serves 4*
2 large aubergines *(eggplant)*
4 courgettes
1 large onion chopped
2 cloves garlic crushed *(optional)*
2 (325g) tins plum tomatoes juice drained
2 bay leaves
1 teaspoon oil
1 glass dry white wine
This is very good cooked in a slow cooker.
First heat oil in a deep a pan, then add
onion and garlic. Chop aubergines into
small squares, slice courgettes in thin slices.
Add the wine and then aubergines, courgettes, tomatoes, bay leaves, some freshly
milled black pepper and a little salt. Add
the water to nearly cover. Cook slowly
until the aubergines are soft. You can cook

it faster but you need to stir often and the vegetables tend to break up. *Serve hot with rice or baked potato or alone as a first course.*

Desserts and cakes

Low calorie pastry
For one 20cm tart or flan case
175g wholemeal or plain flour
1 tablespoon soya flour *(if you can't find this add more plain)*
Pinch salt
1½ teaspoons baking powder
1 tablespoon sunflower oil
Skimmed milk to mix
Sift all the dry ingredients into a large mixing bowl. Add the oil and then enough milk to make a soft dough. The pastry should be left in a cool place for 10-15 minutes before using.

Treacle tart   serves 6
This tart can never be ideal diet food as a large percentage of the calories are in the treacle. How can you have treacle tart without treacle? There is less fat in this recipe and slightly less treacle than usual.
100g low calorie pastry *(see recipe)*

1 untreated lemon
50g fresh breadcrumbs
160ml golden syrup
Make a 20cm tart case with the pastry and bake blind. Grate the zest of the lemon then squeeze the juice and reserve. Put the lemon juice and zest into a pudding bowl over a saucepan of boiling water. Add the golden syrup little by little stirring all the time. Finally stir in the breadcrumbs and mix well. Spread the mixture over the base of the cooled pastry case. Cook in a preheated oven for 25 minutes.
Eat with low fat greek yoghurt.

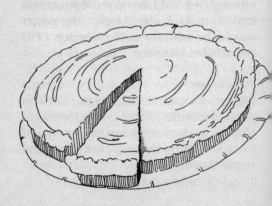

Strawberry pavlova
3 egg whites
125g castor sugar
1 level teaspoon cornflour
1 level teaspoon vinegar
Vanilla essensce
Pinch salt
Very low fat creme fraiche
250g fresh strawberries, washed, hulled and cut in half
Fresh lemon juice
1 banana *(optional)*

Toss the strawberry havles and banana slices *(if using)* in the lemon juice to prevent discolouring. Beat egg whites until stiff and standing in peaks. Add the salt and beat in half sugar fold in rest of sugar and cornflour. Add 1 level teaspoon vinegar and few drops of vanilla essence. Put greaseproof paper on a baking tray and lightly grease. Spoon mixture into middle of paper and spread out evenly making a flat pancake about 3cm thick. Cook in preheated oven 120C for 1-1½ hours. Turn oven off and let meringue cool in oven. Put the base upside down on a pretty plate and just before serving spread creme fraiche on the upper side of the meringue base. Ar-

range the strawberries and slices of banana
in a pattern over the pavlova.

*If you make this with double whipped cream
and tinned fruit in syrup it is very fattening.
There is very little fat in this recipe and remark-
ably few calories. Vary fruit – try raspberries
or tinned fruits in juice. Don't be tempted to
use another cream.*

Raspberry mousse   serves 8

1 packet raspberry or strawberry sugar
free jelly
300ml boiling water
300g very low fat fromage frais
300g fresh or frozen raspberries

Dissolve the jelly in the boiling water and
let this cool but not set. Reserve some fruit
for decoration and blend the fromage frais
and fruit together with the jelly. Pour into
small dishes and leave ot set. Decorate
with a little fruit before eating.

*You can use yellow jelly and fresh pineapple or
green jelly and kiwi fruit. Sugar free jelly has
virtually no calories and very low fat fromage
frais is indeed very low fat.*

Bakewell tart   serves 4-6

100g low calorie pastry *(see recipe)*
2 eggs

100g fresh *not dry* breadcrumbs
2 tablespoons blackberry or raspberry jam
75g granulated sugar
75g ground almonds
1 untreated lemon
salt
1 tablespoon melted butter

Line a 20cm tart case with the pastry. Lightly prick the base of the tart and spread the jam over it. Grate the zest of the lemon and then squeeze the juice and reserve. Beat the egg yolks together in a large mixing bowl and add the breadcrumbs, melted butter and lemon juice, stir together and add the almonds and grated zest of the lemon. Mix well. Beat the egg whites with a pinch of salt until they stand up in little peaks. Gently fold the egg whites into the almond and breadcrumb mixture and spread over the base of the tart. Cook in a preheated oven 220C for 35 minutes.

This tart has less calories due to the pastry. If you wish to further reduce the calories decrease the ground almonds and replace with more breadcrumbs mixed with some almond essence.

Chocolate ice cream

Never feel deprived on a diet again. The chocolaholics will love this low calorie, low fat ice cream. Use this recipe to make delicious 'cheat' ice cream.

1 packet chocolate mouse mix made up according to the instructions with semi skimmed milk *(skimmed milk doesn't work satisfactorily as it becomes too thin)*. Place in a freezer tray. Put the mousse in the freezer and about an hour later you have delicous light chocolate ice cream – beware it needs to be eaten fast!

*You could try this with strawberry mousse too. For children under 5 you **must** make this with full fat milk.*

78

Black cherry cheesecake   serves 4-6

1 tin pitted black cherries in juice
1 packet sugar free blackcurrant jelly
1 small carton very low fat black cherry yoghurt
100g crushed disgestive biscuits
400g 0% fat fromage blanc
300ml boiling water

Dissolve the jelly in the boiling water and leave to cool but not set. Line a loose bottomed cake tin with the crushed biscuits and press down firmly. Drain all the juice from the tin of cherries, reserve a few for decoration and put the rest in a blender. Take a couple of tablespoons of the jelly mixture and mix with the blended cherries. Now spread this mixture over the biscuit base. When the jelly mixture is cool, whisk the yoghurt and the fromage blanc. Pour this into the cake tin and chill until set. Remove from the tin and decorate with a few cherries.

You can reduce the calories further here by using lower calorie biscuits for the base. You can also make it without the tinned black cherries, using more yoghurt and less fromage blanc.

Lemon scones   *12 scones*
225g plain flour
1 teaspoon salt
50g castor sugar
1 teaspoon bicarbonate of soda
grated zest of ½ untreated lemon
25g margarine
140ml low fat yoghurt
semi skimmed milk
In a large mixing bowl place the flour, salt, sugar, bicarbonate of soda, and grated zest of lemon. Rub in the margarine. Then stir in the yoghurt – when you have a soft dough roll it out about 1cm thick. Cut out your scones with a cutter or moistened upturned glass, and place on a baking tray. Brush the scones with a little of the milk and place in a preheated oven 220C for 10-15 minutes.

Do not load these scones with butter, try some low fat spread or even a little lemon curd without butter. You can make them plain if you prefer.

Christmas pudding
This christmas pudding has a much lower fat content than the usual recipes mainly because of the lack of suet. It does not keep well and

should be made no more than a week before christmas

500g breadcrumbs *(wholemeal are best)*
250g sultanas
200g currants
100g chopped mixed peel
4 glace cherries, cut in half
150g peeled, cored apple *(grated)*
100g mixed brazil and hazel nuts *(chopped)*
25g chopped almonds
225g dark demerara sugar
1 untreated lemon for juice and rind
3 eggs
1 teaspoon salt
350ml skimmed milk
1 tablespoon mixed spice

Toss the grated apple in the lemon juice and add the grated zest of the lemon. Lightly beat the eggs together. Put all the dry ingredients into a mixing bowl and mix thoroughly. Add the lemon juice, egg and milk and stir well. Put the mixture into a 2.25 litre pudding bowl, or two smaller ones and cover with greaseproof paper. Tie this around the top with string and steam the pudding for 3 hours. Cool. Keep cool and dry until christmas day. Heat the pudding by steaming for at least an hour.

Low calorie brandy butter   serves 4
Low fat spreads are a disappointing alternative
for brandy butter – but try this delicious low fat
alternative
6 tablespoons of very low fat creme fraiche
1 tablespoon best brandy
Slowly stir the brandy into the creme fraiche
and you have a wonderful accompani-
ment to your christmas pudding.

Mango and passion fruit sorbet
                                    serves 4
2 ripe mangoes
1 passion fruit
1 tablespoon sugar
2 tablespoons water
Slowly dissolve sugar and water on low
heat to make a syrup. Cool. Liquidise the
syrup with the mango and passion fruit
pulp. Freeze. After 2 hours check the
sorbet – if crystallized take it out, stir and
refreeze.
Serious dieters should not eat more than 2
scoops of ice creams or sorbets.

Apple pie
It is not the apple in apple pie which is fattening,
but the pie part – and the custard which goes

with it. Here are low fat alternatives.

650g cooking apples, peeled and cored

juice and grated zest of ½ untreated lemon

3 tablespoon water

½ teaspoon ground cinnamon

2 cloves

75g brown sugar

Low calorie pastry *(see recipe)*

Butter paper

Cut the apples into slices and toss in the lemon juice. Place them in layers in the pie dish, sprinkling the sugar and cinnamon on each layer. Nestle the cloves amongst the apple slices and pour over the water. Lightly grease the rim of your pie dish with the butter paper and roll out your pastry. Cover the pie dish and make a few holes in the pastry. You should have enough pastry trimmings to make a few leaves or apples as decoration. Brush the pastry with semi skimmed milk and bake in a preheated oven 200C for 15 minutes and then reduce the heat to 180C and bake for a further 30 minutes. The pie should be golden brown when ready. Eat hot or cold.

Instead of cream try this:

1 tablespoon very low fat yoghurt per person mixed with 1 teaspoon skimmed milk powder per person. Put a spoonful next to the pie on the plate and trail a little runny honey across it. You can use sweet, eating, apples instead of cooking apples and reduce the amount of sugar in the recipe.

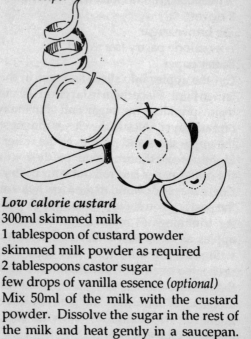

Low calorie custard
300ml skimmed milk
1 tablespoon of custard powder
skimmed milk powder as required
2 tablespoons castor sugar
few drops of vanilla essence *(optional)*
Mix 50ml of the milk with the custard powder. Dissolve the sugar in the rest of the milk and heat gently in a saucepan. Add the rest of the milk slowly stirring all the time. When the custard starts to boil

reduce the heat and simmer for 5 minutes. Add the vanilla if required. If the custard seems too thin stir in some skimmed milk powder to thicken it.

You can further reduce the calories here by using artificial sweetener instead of sugar. Eat with hot apple pie.

Pancakes   makes 4
50g plain flour
Pinch of salt
1 egg
65ml skimmed milk
4 tablespoons water
Juice of 1 lemon
Sprinkling castor sugar
Make the batter early and leave it to rest for a while before making the pancakes. Sift flour and salt into a mixing bowl, lightly beat the egg and make a well in the centre of the flour to hold it. Mix together thoroughly then add the water and the milk slowly beating all the time until smooth. If it is too thick add a little more water. Lightly oil a thick frying pan with sunflower oil and make the pancakes from the batter. Keep warm while you cook the rest and when ready to serve add the

lemon juice together with a sprinkling of sugar.

Chocolate pancakes
makes 4

For a special treat try these delicious pancakes with a low calorie chocolate filling

4 pancakes, made as above *(no lemon juice)*
150ml low fat fromage frais
1 tablespoon castor sugar
1 tablespoon cocoa powder

Place the fromage frais in a small pan, stir in the sugar and cocoa powder and heat very gently until the sugar has melted - *do not boil.*   When you have cooked all 4 pancakes pour some chocolate sauce on each, roll up the pancake and serve.

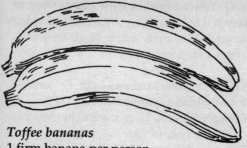

Toffee bananas
1 firm banana per person
Enough granulated white sugar to cover
the base of thick bottomed pan
Juice of ½ lemon
Peel the bananas and slice them in thin
rounds. Toss in the lemon juice to prevent
discolouring. Get a very thick bottomed
pan and cover the base of the pan with
about 1cm of sugar shake gently to get an
even covering. Put pan over the lowest
heat possible. Until the sugar melts. Do
not stir. If one spot melts before the rest
turn the pan around. Arrange banana
slices on a large plate. When sugar is
melted quickly dribble it over the bananas
in a crisscross pattern.
*You can prepare the bananas early and keep in
the lemon juice in the fridge. The toffee is best
prepared at the last minute unless you like it*

soft. *You can sprinkle a few drops of liqueur over just before serving. A teaspoon or 2 of low fat yoghurt or creme fraiche beside the banans makes a memorable dessert.*

The ten minute birthday cake   serves 8
1 ready made sponge flan case
Enough thick low fat creme fraiche to evenly cover the base of flan
Tin stoned stewed black cherries in juice or low sugar cherry pie filling
fresh pineapple *or* fresh or dried and soaked apricots
Spread creme fraiche over the base of the flan case drain juice from tinned fruit and put to one side. Make a circle around the inside edge of the flan with the stewed cherries. Make the initial letter of the lucky birthday person with cherries or cherry pie filling being careful not to smudge it. Gently arrange pieces of pineapple or apricot around the edge of the flan. *Candles in and you are ready to go. It really only takes ten minutes!*
You cannot make this cake too long in advance. But it is so quick that you can make it during the last 'pass the parcel'. For an adult version mix some of the cherry juice with a teaspoon or

2 of liqueur and pour this on the plate before you put the flan case on, this way the juice and liqueur soaks up into the flan. Remember, children under five shoud not have the low fat creme fraiche, give them the real thing and don't be tempted to eat it for them!

Chocolate walnut cake   *serves 6*
50g self raising flour
½ teaspoon baking powder
40g cocoa
20g chopped walnuts
225g demerara sugar
25g butter
2 whole eggs, beaten
75g soft cheese
Grated zest 1 untreated lemon
For the filling:
150ml fromage frais
1 desertspoon castor sugar
1 desertspoon cocoa powder
Put the sifted flour, baking powder and cocoa in a bowl and add the orange zest, nuts and sugar. In another bowl beat together the cheese and butter. Beat this into the dry ingredients. Stir in the beaten eggs until you have an even mixture. Pour into a greased cake tin and bake for 50 minutes

in a preheated oven, 180C. To make the filling stir the castor sugar and cocoa powder into the fromage frais. When the cake is cool, cut in half, spread the filling on one half, cover with the other half and decorate with a light sprinkling of cocoa powder on the top.

Rice pudding with almonds　　　*serves 4*
1 litre skimmed milk
110g short grain pudding rice
sugar to taste, 1-2 tablespoons
1 vanilla pod split *or* few drops essence
1 tablespoon flaked almonds
Wash the rice then soak in the milk for ½ hour. Bring rice and milk to the boil with sugar, and split vanilla pod stirring all the time. Reduce heat and simmer for 40 minutes. Remove the vanilla pod *(if using)*. Toast the almonds, by putting in a frying pan over a very low heat, turn from time to time and when starting to brown remove from heat. Serve this pudding in small bowls with a few almonds on top.
To further reduce the calories replace some or all of the sugar with artificial sweetener and leave out the almonds

Pear sorbet
300g fresh pears, skin and core removed, *or* tinned, juice drained
100g castor sugar
½ pint water *or* syrup from the tin
2 egg whites
For fresh fruit heat sugar and water to make a syrup. Cool and put aside. Simmer chopped fresh fruit with a tablespoon of water until soft. Cool, put fruit and syrup in blender. If using tinned, put contents straight into blender. Blend and freeze until firm. Beat egg whites until stiff then fold in fruit mixture. Freeze once more until firm.

You can make this sorbet with any fruit. Most calories here are in the sugar but you need to make the syrup to stop the sorbet freezing too hard. Sorbet is a low fat alternative to ice cream. Try making savoury sorbets too, skinned and deseeded tomatoes are easy and cucumber is delicious.

Strawberry ice cream
fresh or frozen strawberries
very low fat creme fraiche *(½ weight of fruit)*
2 tablespoons sugar per 500g fruit
2 tablespoons water per 500g fruit
Cook fruit in water and sugar until soft. Let mixture cool and liquidise long enoug to mash up fruit but not lose the texture. Add creme fraiche *(you can use half low fat yoghurt)*. Freeze this mixture *(it will freeze in ice making compartment)*. Let ice cream soften a bit in the fridge about ½ hour before serving.

Sauces and dressings
Celery and ham sauce   *serves 4*
Excellent with grilled turkey or veal escalopes
1 head celery
1 tablespoon white wine *(optional)*
125ml pot natural low fat yoghurt

---

1 teaspoon dried skimmed milk powder
100g sliced ham trimmed of fat and cut into
matchsticks
1 tablespoon finely chopped parsley
salt and freshly ground black pepper
Clean celery and remove the tips. Pull off
any tough strings then cut stalks into little
chunks about 1-2cm wide. Cook in boiling
slightly salted water for about 15 minutes,
drain most of the water and add the wine,
yoghurt, powdered milk and ham. Season
with parsley and black pepper. Heat and
smother the escalopes. Serve with broccoli
and potatoes or rice.

This sauce goes well with noodles too if you add
a little more ham.

Low calorie white sauce
1 tablespoon rice flour
300ml skimmed milk
Black pepper and salt
Mix the rice flour and a little milk to a paste in a saucepan and stir in the rest of the milk. Bring to the boil and simmer for 5 minutes. Season with pepper and salt. Add fresh finely chopped herbs or mustard.

Low calorie mayonnaise
125ml low fat plain yoghurt
125ml 0% fat creme fraiche
1 teaspoon dijon mustard
1 teaspoon wine vinegar
black pepper and salt
fresh crushed garlic
5 drops sesame oil *(optional)* this makes it delicious, but it is still good without
Mix the vinegar, mustard and seasoning together first then slowly add the yoghurt and creme fraiche stirring all the time. One way to decrease the fat of ordinary mayonnaise is to make it as usual but use a whole egg instead of just the egg yolk. The mayonnaise is much lighter and you use less oil than ordinary mayonnaise.

Low calorie blue cheese dressing
Good on salads or jacket potatoes
2 tablespoons danish blue cheese
4 tablespoons very low fat creme fraiche *or*
fromage blanc
Freshly ground black pepper
Skimmed milk
Mix the creme fraiche and blue cheese until
smooth. Add the pepper and then the
skimmed milk to make it as runny or thick
as you wish.

Low calorie salad dressing
1 teaspoon red wine vinegar *(raspberry*
flavoured is delicious)
1 teaspoon dijon mustard
Black pepper
1 teaspoon olive oil
Low fat plain yoghurt
Mix everything together except the oil and
the yoghurt. Beat in the oil until the mixture looks slightly thick. Add the yoghurt
slowly until you have enough dressing.
Add more mustard or vinegar if you wish.
This dressing is very good on salad after pasta
if you add some oregano and spring onion or
shallot chopped very small to the first mixture

THE ESSENTIAL SERIES

Essential Tum & Bum Diet
by Mandy Roberts & Ariane Castaing
Shed the pounds from your tum & bum in mouth-watering style. Packed full of health and diet tips.

Essential Tum & Bum Exercises
by Becca Thompson
These easy, clearly illustrated, exercises will quickly tone those stubborn tum & bum areas.

Essential Low Calorie Treats
by Mandy Roberts
These low calorie dishes are a treat for all the family – a perfect supplement to a low fat diet.

Essential Fat & Cholesterol Counter
by Anthea Nichols
This definitive counter will help you plan a healthy low fat diet for your family.

Essential Low Fat & Cholesterol Diet
by Dr Amanda Roberts
Avoid heart disease by altering your eating habits – this book shows you how in mouthwatering style

Essential Vitamin Book
by Caroline Berry
The definitive guide to which foods contain what vitamins and how they work for us.

Essential First Aid
by Dr Amanda Roberts
With clear instructions, this illustrated guide enables you to deal quickly with any emergency.

Available from bookshops or direct from
Boatswain Press Ltd
12 North Street, Emsworth, Hants PO10 7DQ